The Pope in Chicago

An Album of Photographs, Artwork, and Text Commemorating the Visit of Pope John Paul II to Chicago in October, 1979

Follett Publishing Company, Chicago

Dirck Halstead — Black Star

"The papal presence among us is a source of great spiritual blessings and renewal for the Archdiocese of Chicago. The members of all religious faiths of this important metropolitan area have expressed through us their delight that he has come again to visit. May God's blessing be upon him in his worldwide work f peace, justice and charity."

—John Cardinal C•

"Habemus Papam!"

The white smoke hardly had time to puff or wisp or swirl above the Sistine Chapel chimney before the steady breeze made it disappear into the Roman hills the evening of October 16, 1978.

To linger much longer, however, was the shock which followed that traditional signal that the Roman Catholic Church had a new pope.

Surprise . . . and then quickly, joy . . . claimed the crowd below in St. Peter's Square and the millions in front of television sets the world over when the voice from the basilica balcony announced, "Habemus Papam!" We have a pope! And then the name: Karol Wojtyla, a Polish cardinal, had been elected to lead the Church.

They had done it! The Sacred College of Cardinals—those 111 red-garbed princes of the Church—had broken with a 455-year tradition and elected a non-Italian pope.

Who is this man who asked to be called Pope John Paul II, this man for whom the Italian papal legacy had been overturned?

Karol Wojtyla, Pope John Paul II, is an actor, a poet, a politician, a theologian, a philospher, a teacher of ethics; yet he is a teaser, a joker, quick with the wit and ever with the wink. Moreover, he is a defender of religious freedom, a man of the people and a man of nerves. And, above all, he is a man of God.

"It is not permissible to transform man into a robot. Man is greater than all the calculations planned for the economy."

In a traditional photo from the late 1920s, little Karol Wojtyla poses after making his First Holy Communion.

Born May 18, 1920 in a town in southern Poland, Wadowice, Karol Wojtyla wasn't sure he wanted to be a priest until he had already started college at Cracow's Jagiellonian University. He was active in the theater group there and wrote poetry.

When the Nazis overran Poland at the start of World War II, Karol Wojtyla worked in a quarry and later in a chemical factory while secretly he studied for the priesthood. A Nazi prohibition had driven the Cracow seminary underground.

He was ordained a Catholic priest in 1946 and sent to Rome's Angelicum College where he earned a doctorate in philosophy. His return to Poland as a parish priest in 1948 coincided with the rise to power of its Kremlin-controlled communist government.

In those early years of his priesthood he counseled students while teaching ethics at Jagiellonian University. Later he held the chair of ethics at the Catholic University of Lublin, Eastern Europe's only non-state college. But Father Wojtyla was meant for greater responsibilities.

In 1958, at the relatively youthful age of 38, he was made an auxiliary bishop of Cracow. Within four years he was the Apostolic Administrator of the See and by 1964 he was named an archbishop.

The post called for a special man, one who had to lead an overwhelmingly Catholic population (95 percent) in a state which denied and still denies the existence of God in its official policy. Archbishop Wojtyla proved he was not awed by the communists.

He criticized the government repeatedly as he attempted to protect the human rights of Poland's citizens, and he was vehement in his struggle to have the government remove its restrictions on religious education. At the Second Vatican Council he exhorted the leaders of the Catholic Church to make a ceaseless effort to secure religious liberty throughout the world.

Pope Paul VI raised Archbishop Wojtyla to the College of Cardinals in the same consistory where Chicago's Archbishop John Cody became a cardinal in 1967. And Cracow's archbishop continued to use the power of the faith of the Polish people to win grudging but unavoidable concessions from the communist government. As late as 197_ he was chiding, "It is not permissible to transform man into a robot," when the government tried to force miners to work on Sunday and miss attending Mass. "Man is greater than all the calculations planned for the economy," he said. "Can we speak of national unity when there are people in our society with all the qualifications for becoming directors of a mine or a foundry, but are told, 'You can have the job when you give up being a believer'?"

It was such a spirit which moved the College of Cardinals to choose the Polish church leader in the second papal election in two months follow_

The Pope is no stranger to Chicago, having visited the city twice before as the Archbishop of Cracow in Poland, once in 1969 and again (pictured) in 1976. On both occasions he slept in the rectory at Five Holy Martyrs Parish in the city's heavily Polish Brighton Park neighborhood. The previous visits were good-will tours, and Cardinal Wojtyla even viewed the city from the Sears Skydeck and took a boat cruise along the lakefront.

ng the sudden fatal heart attack of Pope John Paul I. The Archbishop of Cracow was the man to sit in the Chair of St. Peter. "Papa Wojtyla" reassured the Italian faithful of his devotion to the whole Church.

"I am speaking to you in your... our Italian language," the Polish native said from St. Peter's balcony immediately after his election. And then the wit showed: "If I make a mistake, correct me."

Since then, John Paul II has created a new kind of papacy.

This pope swims, skis, canoes, hikes, dances with young people, holds campfires at Castelgandolfo, joins in songfests, and kids with former Chicagoan and ardent golfer, Bishop Aloysius Wycislo of Green Bay, Wisconsin, "It's Polish to follow a white ball around. Why don't you learn to ski?"

In his first year as pope, he wrote an encyclical, "Redemptor Hominis" (The Redeemer of Man), criticizing totalitarian regimes, the arms race, and what he called "the consumer civilization."

And Pope John Paul II showed his traditional background by reaffirming the Catholic policy of unmarried priests.

That traditionalism surfaced again in Mexico where more progressive Catholics took offense at the Pontiff's refusal to endorse "liberation theology" as the answer for Latin America's woes.

But not even controversial stands on priestly celibacy and laicization for priests has dimmed the enthusiasm of the world for this 263rd successor to St. Peter. Weekly general audiences had to be moved outdoors when crowds of 70,000 became too much for the 15,000-seat papal audience hall, audiences which create traffic jams every Wednesday in Rome. Millions turned out to catch a glimpse of Pope John Paul II on his travels to Mexico and Poland earlier this year.

When Cardinal Cody (left) and Chicago Auxiliary Bishop Alfred Abramowicz (right) paid a return visit to Poland in 1977, then Cardinal Wojtyla joined them in laying a wreath and praying at the Auschwitz death camp.

He has become a pope who is still a priest, who married an Italian couple and baptized a British baby. And he has shown he is still a man with everyday feelings.

When thousands of Polish students gathered to sing "Sto lat" ("One hundred years—may you live one hundred years!") outside his residence on the trip to Poland, Pope John Paul opened the window and asked, "Do you really want the Pope to live one hundred years?"

When the crowd shouted, "Yes!", the Pope quipped, "Well, then, let him get some sleep."

"Eminence, not too long, Eminence," whispered Chicago priest Father John Rolek as the then Archbishop of Cracow, Karol Cardinal Wojtyla, rose to preach before a standing crowd of 250,000 at Jasna Gora on the Feast of Our Lady of Czestochowa in 1977. Afterwards he asked, "How long was I, Johnny?" Told that his sermon with the pilgrims from Chicago in the audience lasted but 22 minutes, Cardinal Wojtyla winked and whispered, "Not too bad, not too bad."

Commemorative Album 1979

The Pope in Chicago

PORTRAITS AND ART SUITABLE FOR FRAMING

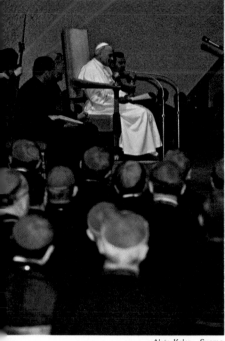

Alain Keler — Sygma

Pope John XXIII surprised the world by calling for an ecumenical council to renew the Roman Catholic Church. He had been Pope for merely ninety days when he made the announcement in January, 1959. Attending the Second Vatican Council were people with names which would become part of papal history later, men named Karol Wojtyla, Albino Luciani, and Giovanni Montini.

"Good Pope John" would not live to see his council to its conclusion, however, and Cardinal Montini was elected to oversee the final outcome and to lead the post-conciliar Church as Pope Paul VI.

It was a trying fifteen years, years of great tension among Catholics as their Church went through Vatican II growing pains. Upon the death of Paul VI in August, 1978, the Sacred College of Cardinals selected Cardinal Luciani to follow.

As Pope John Paul I he won the nickname "the smiling Pope," but the smiles ended all too soon. Death came only 34 days after he took up the papacy. However his name—a combination of the two popes who had preceded him—lived on after the second papal conclave of 1978.

Not since 1523 had a pope—Adrian VI of Holland—come from anywhere besides Italy when Karol Cardinal Wojtyla was elected and chose to be called Pope John Paul II. During the Mass celebrating the beginning of his ministry, the new Pope asked the faithful: "Pray for me! Help me to be able to serve you."

Fabian — Sygma

The newly-installed Pope John Paul II greets a group from the Chicago Catholic League in Rome. Included are Sister Caroline of St. Casimir's Parish and Miss June Grabowski, national secretary of the Catholic League.

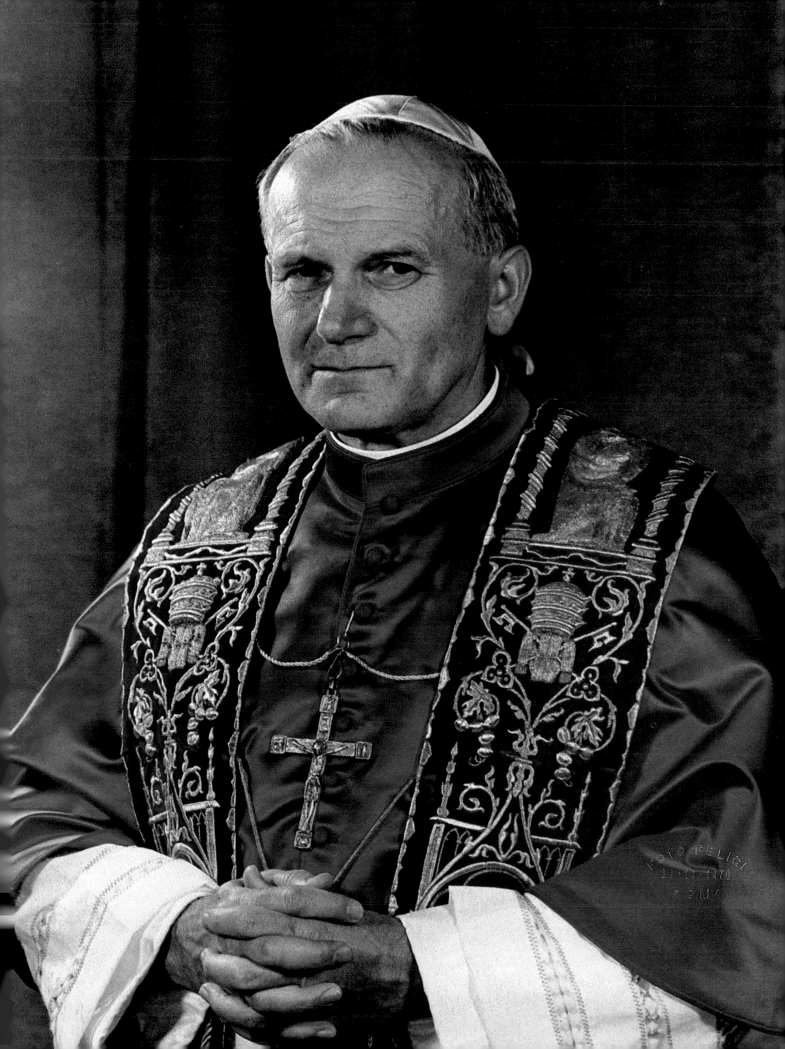

A Traveling Pope

After centuries when the popes were virtual prisoners in the Vatican, Pope John Paul II immediately took his papacy outside the walls of Vatican City.

Within his first year as pope he traveled to Mexico, his native Poland, Ireland, and the United States. But John Paul II has not been one to sit idly around St. Peter's between his major travels. He has made it a point to offer Mass as often as his schedule permits in the neighborhood churches of Rome.

As Pope he has visited Assisi, the home of saintly Francis. Another trip took him to Nettuno, the home town of St. Maria Goretti. In honor of his predecessor, Pope John Paul I, he visited Albino Luciani's birthplace, Canale d'Agordo. He donned a fur-lined cap to bless a statue of the Madonna during a driving snowstorm in the Italian alps near Belluno.

The new Pope visits Assisi, home of St. Francis.

Claudio Marcelli — Sygma

Dressed in mitre, Pope John Paul II greets the crowd at Mexico's Shrine of Our Lady of Guadalupe.

Michael Norcia — Sygma

Crowds line the streets as far as the eye can see for the Panama-hatted Pope as he motorcades through Guadalajara.

Diego Goldberg — Sygma

"Viva Papa! Viva Mexico!"

The first trip of the new Pope outside of Italy was to attend the Third General Conference of the Latin American Bishops held in Puebla, Mexico in January. He was the first Pope ever to visit that country and won the hearts of the people by kneeling to kiss the soil upon his arrival. Officials estimated that some 5 million people lined the route of the motorcade through the streets of Mexico City to the cathedral where he celebrated Mass and delivered a homily in Spanish. Crowds shouted "Viva Papa! Viva Mexico!" wherever he went. Before the Puebla conference, he concelebrated Mass with all the bishops at the Basilica of Our Lady of Guadalupe. In Oaxaca he met with the Indians of the region, confering ministries of lector and acolyte on ten of them. Before Mexico he stopped in the Dominican Republic and afterwards in Nassau before returning to Rome.

Goldberg — Sygma

Michael Norcia — Sygma

Facing page: The Pope celebrated Mass at the beautiful Altar of the Kings in the Cathedral of Mexico, oldest and largest in Latin America. Painting by Chicago artist-reporter Franklin McMahon.

A Son of Poland Returns

With Stephan Cardinal Wyszynski, primate of Poland, Karol Wojtyla returns as Pope John Paul II to his homeland.

C. Simonpietri — Sygma

The visit of Pope John Paul II to Poland was a natural return to his homeland. The Pontiff would not let the Polish faithful forget—as Polish government authorities would have liked—that his visit was also a celebration of the 900th anniversary of the martyrdom of St. Stanislaus, patron saint of Poland, who was killed for disagreeing with the king.

In a nation officially atheist by its policy, millions openly prayed with the Polish Pope as he traveled through Warsaw, Crakow, and his home town of Wadowice. In windows throughout Poland, Catholics blatantly displayed their faith by hanging paper cut-outs of the papal tiara and Pope John Paul II's coat of arms. And few Christians and non-Christians will forget the touching scenes as he knelt before the walls of Auschwitz and when he received the greeting of prison-stripe-clad survivors of the Nazi concentration camp there.

Facing page: The Pope enters Auschwitz through the gate with the ironic greeting "Arbeit Macht Frei" (Work Will Make Free). Painting by Chicago artist-reporter Franklin McMahon

Henri Bureau — Sygma

The First Pop

Henri Bureau — Sygma

Banners strung across the front of this church in Poland honor Christ and Mary.

C. Simonpietri — Sygma

On his way to Chicago in Octobe
Pope John Paul II stopped in Ireland f
a three-day visit, the first time a pop
had ever been there. He participated
the 100th anniversary celebration of th
apparition of the Blessed Virgin Ma
at the town of Knock.

The Pontiff stopped briefly in Bosto
offering Mass on Boston Common b
fore traveling to New York where h
addressed the United Nations Gener
Assembly. The Holy Father celebrate
public Masses in New York at Yank
Stadium and Battery Park, on Philade
phia's Benjamin Franklin Parkway ar
in Des Moines, Iowa, each with a pa
ticular theme which echoed a conce
of the Polish Pope. Then, early evenir
on October 4, he arrived in Chicago, th
first pope ever to visit the Windy Cit

Martha Leonard — Mayor's Office

Welcome!

Joannes Paulus pp II

COPERNICUS CIVIC-CULTURAL CENTER

To the city of the nation's largest Roman Catholic archdiocese, to the city having the greatest American population of citizens of his own nativity, to a city where all people, of every creed, have eagerly awaited him, I am privileged to welcome the Holy Father, Pope John Paul II.

For Pope John Paul II, this visit will be his third to Chicago, his previous appearances having been as Cardinal Wojtyla in 1969 and 1976. Civic-minded as we are, we would like to think that he liked Chicago so well that he was determined to return. It was surely not foreseen at that time that he would come to us as the head of his Church, a world religious leader who has become, in the comparatively short time of his pontificate, universally admired and beloved.

As John Cardinal Cody has stated, the Pope's visit is a joyous event, a spiritual experience unprecedented, and as Mayor of Chicago, on behalf of all of its people, I extend to the Holy Father the heartiest of welcomes.

—Jane M. Byrne
Mayor

This 18k gold paperweight was one of the gifts from the city to the Pope. Designed by Michigan Avenue jeweler Lester Lampert, it is valued at $10,000.00, paid for by prominent Chicagoans.

After thanking the pilot for a safe journey from Des Moines, Pope John Paul II walked down the ramp from Shepherd I to the applause of a thousand invited guests. The sound of 30 violins from students of the Suzuki Academy of the Performing Arts serenaded his arrival, one and a half hours late. "He loves people," said one enthusiastic observer, "that's why he's late." It was hard to leave the cheering throngs in Iowa. Mayor Jane Byrne, wearing a black lace mantilla, kissed his ring and said the Polish word for "Greeting," learned for the occasion. After a short five-minute walk to a limousine, surrounded by bishops and Secret Service agents, he drove off with Cardinal Cody for the motorcade to Holy Name Cathedral.

Governor James Thompson welcomed the Pope on behalf of the 11 million citizens of Illinois.

Mayor Byrne said children were among the invited guests at the airport "because he loves children." They presented him with flowers and he blessed and hugged them before moving on carrying a single red rose.

Crowds waited patiently for the Pope's motorcade from O'Hare Airport to come along Milwaukee Avenue in a predominently Polish section.

The Progress Band practices for the Pope's arrival. The girl in front is in traditional Polish dress.

Students along Milwaukee Avenue dressed warmly for the long wait.

The Knights of Columbus provided a colorful honor guard for the Pope's Friday night visit to St. Peter's Church in the Loop. There he addressed Franciscan and other brothers, recalling their vows to follow Jesus in poverty, chastity, and obedience.

wo of the faithful find a ood vantage from a ilwaukee Avenue porch.

Students from Resurrection High School cheered with the crowds when the papal motorcade went by, too fast for them.

Two Polish survivors of the Nazi concentration camps were especially eager to greet the Pope on Milwaukee Avenue.

The predominantly Polish neighborhood was festooned with balloons as well as banners, posters, and papal portraits.

"... a witness ... among the most needy ...."

Early arrivals waited for Pope John Paul in the pre-dawn darkness at 18th and Union for his visit to the Pilsen neighborhood.

Always a port of entry for immigrants, Chicago's Pilsen neighborhood was chosen for a stop on Pope John Paul's itinerary because the Pilsen Housing and Business Alliance receives support through the Campaign for Human Development, the poverty-fighting, self-help program of the Catholic Church in the United States. He called the Campaign's work "a witness to the Church's living presence in the world among the most needy." The Pope accepted bouquets of flowers given to him by children from the Providence of God Parish where his open-topped limousine stopped in the now Hispanic neighborhood. He also greeted diocesan directors of the Campaign from around the country.

Pilsen community members were grateful to the Pope for including them in his Chicago travels, but they made certain he was aware of their needs, too.

Bouquets of flowers are held by community members waiting for the Pope's motorcade to arrive at Providence of God Church.

"Sto Lat, Janie Pawle II"

Representatives selected from Polish-American parishes throughout Chicagoland received Holy Communion from Pope John Paul II when he offered a Polish-language Mass outside Five Holy Martyrs Church on South Richmond Avenue. Comfortable speaking his native language, the pontiff quipped, "The number of Poles has greatly increased since last year," a tongue-in-cheek comment on the aftermath of his election to the papacy. This was the only Mass for Poles that he celebrated during his American trip and 17,000 attended, chosen by lottery at most Polish parishes. Thousands of others watched. The Pope had celebrated Mass at Five Holy Martyrs during his previous two Chicago visits when he was Archbishop of Cracow in Poland. Pastor of the parish is Bishop Alfred Abramowicz, an old friend.

The wall of Five Holy Martyrs School featured a 40-foot high mural of Our Lady of Czestochowa, patroness of Poland.

The Holy Father kissed youngsters dressed in First Communion outfits after they told him, "God loves you," in both Polish and English.

Youngsters formed part of the Living Rosary in the prelude to the papal Mass for the Polish-American community.

Painting by Chicago
artist-reporter
Franklin McMahon.

"...live by faith...."

The Pope traveled to Quigley Preparatory Seminary South in Chicago to meet with more than 350 bishops representing every state in the union. Greeting him when the papal motorcade arrived were, from left, Chicago's John Cardinal Cody, Bishop Thomas Kelly, general secretary of the National Catholic Bishops Conference, Archbishop John Quinn, president of the Bishops Conference, and, being introduced by Archbishop Quinn, Father Gerald Kicanas, rector of Quigley South.

The Pontiff left the seminary by helicopter for Cardinal Cody's residence on the Near North Side to prepare for Mass with the bishops in Grant Park.

The crowd in front of Quigley South received a blessing from the Holy Father as he stood upon the seminary roof. Among the people were many handicapped brought especially for the occasion.

Pope John Paul urged the seminarians at Quigley South to "live by faith even more profoundly." Later, when the students presented him with a soccer ball, he playfully bounced it on the stage.

"Chicago is an American City"

Crowds line the Michigan Avenue Bridge over the Chicago River to see Pope John Paul II as his motorcade drives by.

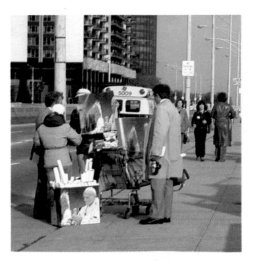

A vendor along Randolph Street near Michigan Avenue offers mementoes of the first-ever visit by a pope to Chicago.

The crowd, estimated upwards of 1.2 million, stretched from Randolph Street below the Standard Oil Building to Buckingham Fountain. They heard the Pope praise the unity of this nation of immigrants in his homily at the Grant Park Mass. "You have traveled 'from sea to shining sea' to find your identity, to discover each other along the way, and to find your place in this immense country."

Buses, parked as far away from Grant Park as the Soldier Field lots, brought worshippers to the Mass from throughout the Midwest.

"One nation... many people"

Although Park District officials had planned not to allow Mass goers to spend the night before the papal liturgy in Grant Park, the order was not enforced, and several people spent Thursday night in sleeping bags in the lakefront park.

Joey McGreevy, 13, of St. John the Evangelist Parish in suburban Streamwood, found one way to see over the Grant Park multitude.

A traditionally-garbed Daughter of St. Paul uses modern photographic equipment to capture candid pictures of the scene in Grant Park.

Youngsters found park trees to be a vantage point.

With Buckingham Fountain splashing in the background, Knights of Columbus formed an honor guard for the Pope at the Grant Park Mass.

More than 350 bishops from North America concelebrated the Grant Park Mass. In his homily there, the Holy Father asked Catholics to remain faithful to church laws. "No local ecclesial community therefore can cut itself off from the treasure of the faith as proclaimed by the Church's teaching office," he said.

Waves of recognition rippled through the crowd as Pope John Paul II came into view at the site of the largest public Mass on his Chicago visit. The Pope called for unity to help spread the Gospel, urging, "Let love then build the bridges across our differences and at times our contrasting positions."

Pope John Paul II gave Holy Communion to 150 persons selected from each of the 12 vicariates, the geographic divisions of the Archdiocese of Chicago. Yellow mums which colored steps on either side of the papal altar were saved to be distributed to Chicagoland shut-ins as mementoes of the Pope's visit.

Left: Chicagoland priests who distributed Holy Communion during the papal Mass pray at the back of the altar.

Below: People from various parts of the Archdiocese who are taking instructions to become Catholics joined in the Rite of Initiation prior to the papal Mass. The service was in keeping with the theme the Pontiff chose for the liturgy, evangelization.

A Symphonic Farewell

After almost 24 hours in Chicago with the demanding schedule that required six different speaking engagements and the celebration of two major liturgies, the music-loving Pope John Paul II was treated to the music of the world-famous Chicago Symphony Orchestra. Georg Solti conducted the symphony in a concert of sacred music at Holy Name Cathedral on the city's Near North Side. Although the concert began in the early evening, the Holy Father arrived later at the intermission. Draperies in the papal colors of yellow and white honored the Pope across the main entrance of the cathedral.

Chicagoland: Where 2.5 Million Catholics Live and Worship

Why should Pope John Paul II choose Chicago as a major stop on his brief visit to the United States?

Its central location made the city a good place for the 350-plus Catholic bishops from around the country to gather and meet with the Holy Father. The fact that Chicago has more Catholics than any other archdiocese in the nation helped, too.

Some 2.5 million Catholics live and worship in Lake and Cook Counties, the areas of Illinois which make up the Archdiocese of Chicago. They participate in liturgical services and social activities in 447 separate parishes, and those 447 local Catholic communities are as diverse in membership, economic wealth, and ethnic makeup as one might expect from so large a group. On any given weekend, Mass is celebrated in 13 different languages in the Archdiocese of Chicago.

Services for the handicapped, widowed and divorced, counseling for troubled marriages, and various parish ministries are housed in the Chicago Archdiocesan Administrative Center at 155 East Superior Street.

St. Joseph Hospital is one of 23 Catholic hospitals in Chicagoland.

Mass inside Holy Name Cathedral, heart of the Chicago archdiocese.

Youngsters gather around the altar for a special Mass for them in the Peoria diocese.

The archdiocese territory stretches along with southwestern tip of Lake Michigan from Zion in the north to Calumet City in the south and includes steel mills and truck farms and factories which manufacture countless items. And the archdiocese has its rural, small town, and suburban parishes.

Chicago itself is known as a city of neighborhoods and in many cases it is the Catholic parish which has been the lifeblood of those neighborhoods. Even non-Catholic residents, when asked where they are from, are likely to answer, "Visitation" or "St. Gabe's."

The Chicago archdiocese opera one of the largest school systems the world—public or private. Six fo year Catholic colleges here draw s dents from around the globe. The Ca olic community supports 23 hospit for Chicagoland, and Catholic Chariti of Chicago provides innumerable s vices to Catholics and non-Cathol alike through homes for the aged a the retarded, in nursing homes, a through its foster parent agency a senior citizen activities.

An important part of Catholic life is the Catholic school. A pupil studies in Springfield, Illinois.

Visiting a prison is part of the ministry of this Milwaukee priest.

A Catholic marriage begins with vows at the altar, as it did for this Peoria diocese couple.

Bishop Edward O'Rourke ordains a deacon for the Diocese of Peoria.

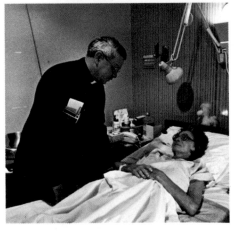

A priest brings the sacraments to a hospital patient in Milwaukee.

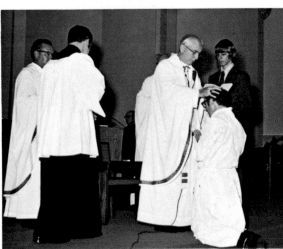

While the Archdiocese of Chicago as spread from the churches of the oop—Old St. Mary's, St. Peter's, and t. Patrick's—out to where a section as cut off to form a new diocese, oliet—what has grown also has been e way the official church tries to help s members.

The archdiocese offers programs to d engaged couples, married men and omen, the separated and the di- rced, youth and the unborn. Its agen- es and departments reach out to the ndicapped, to college students and the underprivileged. It brings the orld of God to others through the mmercial airwaves and through a ulti-million dollar televsion network its own. Many of these programs ich originated in Chicago have be- me models for the rest of the coun- , and the archdiocese continues to be leader in developing ways to help ople live more full and productive es which bring them closer to God.

1926 Eucharistic Congress

Hispanics: A

The visit of Pope John Paul II to Chicago this year with its massive crowds and preparations rivals the Twenty-eighth International Eucharistic Congress held here 52 years ago in 1926, the first such Congress held on U.S. soil. Chicago's George Cardinal Mundelein hosted the Papal Legate, 12 other cardinals, 57 archbishops, 300 bishops, and a million pilgrims from here and throughout the country. The still uncompleted Soldier Field was the site of the opening ceremony and Mass. A 49-step pyramid held the altar at the north end of the stadium, providing greater visibility for people a quarter of a mile away. A 62,000-voice children's choir sang the **Mass of the Angels.** The final meeting of the Congress was at St. Mary of the Lake Seminary at Mundelein with the regal ecclesiastical procession moving solemnly and soddenly through a sudden downpour, drenching them and an estimated one million worshippers.

(Chicago Historical Society photo.)

Maria Marin, Director of the Social Care Program of Maternity B.V.M. Parish, stocks the pantry with food for needy families.

Growing Community

Members representing the Hispanic community around Maternity B.V.M. gather to sing with organist Alfonso Enciso from Colombia before the portrait of Our Lady of Guadalupe. Rafael Romero is from the Cuban community, Paz Zapata and Socorro Dorado are from the Mexican. Others are from Puerto Rico.

Children play in the schoolyard of Maternity B.V.M. parish at 3647 W. North Avenue.

St. Patrick's: The Heart of the Irish

St. Patrick's Church during 1979 Mass on the feast of its patron.

Left: Irish-American John Cardinal Cody celebrated the annual St. Patrick's Day Mass in 1976.

The St. Patrick's Day Parades in Chicago's Loop regularly feature the Irish Christian Brothers and the Pioneer Total Abstinence Society.

Synonymous with being Irish in Chicago is to attend the annual Mass at St. Patrick's Church on St. Patrick's Day. Here the late Mayor Richard J. Daley and Mrs. Eleanor Daley exit from St. Patrick's with Auxiliary Bishop Nevin W. Hayes after the 1974 service.

A Christian Education: From Cradle to College and Beyond

Below, right: The multi-million dollar Catholic Television Network of Chicago (CTN/C) brings programs of interest to area parishes, schools, hospitals, and institutions. "The Word" was a long-running CTN/C series offering suggestions for preparing worship. Here Moderator Father Patrick J. O'Malley interviews Father Vincent Giese.

Bottom, right: DePaul University is in downtown Chicago.

Students from 18 religious communities in this country and abroad attend Catholic Theological Union in Chicago's Hyde Park. Here President Alcuin Coyle, O.F.M. chats with Juan Huitrado from Mexico, Kathleen Sullivan from Chicago, and Fernando de Cabo from Spain. The Jesuit School of Theology headed by William Guindon, S.J., also is in Hyde Park.

Left: Sister Mary Damasia teaches a
course in philosophy to students
at Felician College in the northwest
section of Chicago.

Below: Rosary College is in
River Forest.

Below, left: Mundelein College is on
the northern edge of Chicago.

Bottom, left: Loyola University has
three campuses in the Chicago area.

A Second Homeland for Poles: "Stanislawowo"

Some 850,000 Catholics of Polish descent live in Chicago and its suburbs, and 52 of the Chicago archdiocese's 44 parishes are predominantly Polish today.

When Poles first came to Chicago, it was to the Near Northwest Side that they migrated. After a period when the German and Irish priestly administrators attempted to assimiliate the Poles into existing Catholic parishes, a Polish parish was finally founded in 1870. It was named after Stanislaus Kostka, the Polish boy saint of the sixteenth century.

The recent immigrants naturally leaned toward clergy who could minister and preach to them in their own language, and so it was the Resurrectionist Fathers who were stationed there who climbed to the tower of St. Stanislaus Church to watch the Chicago Fire of 1871.

St. Stanislaus flourished to the point where at one time it counted more than 40,000 parishioners. Some 4,000 children attended the parish school and the faculty numbered 73. Sixty-seven of those were School Sisters of Notre Dame.

The area around St. Stanislaus, near what is now Milwaukee Avenue and Ashland Boulevard, became almost a second homeland for Chicago's Polish-Americans, and they still refer to the neighborhood in the endearing Polish term "Stanislawowo."

St. Stanislaus became the "mother church" of all the Polish parishes in Chicago and the Midwest. When Polish Catholics crowded into St. Stanislaus in such great numbers, a second Polish church, Holy Trinity, was built just two blocks away.

After getting the North Side Poles started, the Resurrectionists secured a Polish-speaking priest for those moving into the Near Southwest Side neighborhood around 17th Street and Paulina Avenue. That led to the founding of St. Adalbert Parish in 1874. Soon the Polish religious order brought its ministry to the Poles working in the steel mills near South Chicago, and Immaculate Conception Church was built. Then it was out to Lemont and LaSalle in Illinois, and to LaPorte and South Bend in Indiana.

In Chicago the growth of the Polish community followed a hopscotching pattern up the diagonals from the downtown area. Poles moved north along Milwaukee Avenue founding parishes such as St. Fidelis, St. Hyacinth, St. Hedwig, St. John Cantius, St. Thecla, and St. Tarcissus.

Along Archer Avenue, the South Side Polish community grew to found St. Barbara, St. Pancratius, Five Holy Martyrs, St. Bruno, and St. Turibius. In the Bridgeport neighborhood, Poles built St. Mary of Perpetual Help, then moved out to the south to establish St. Joseph and St. John of God.

Far right: St. Stanislaus pastor, Father Richard Balazs, C.R., displays an antique chalice from the founding days of the century-old Polish parish

Right: St. Stanislaus Kostka Church

The birthplace of Chicago's Polish-American community lies just beyond the John F. Kennedy Expressway on the city's Near Northwest Side. At Augusta Boulevard and Milwaukee Avenue is the headquarters of the Polish Roman Catholic Union, an important Polish fraternal society. The twin steeples belong to Holy Trinity Church, the second oldest Polish church in Chicago.

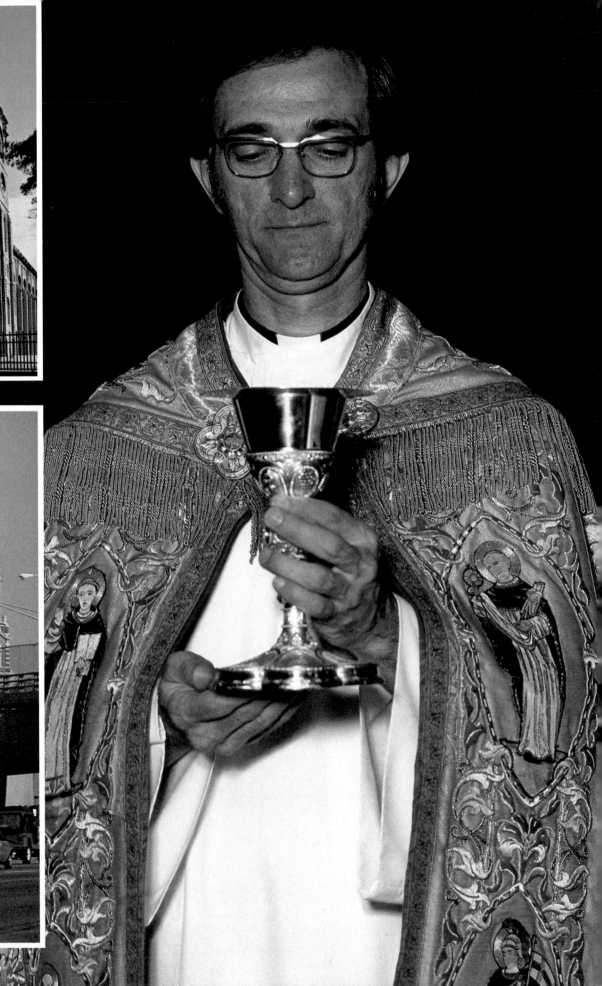

Above, left: Inside St. Stanislaus Church

Above: This "Fiddleback" chasuble is from a collection of vestments used in the early years of St. Stanislaus Church, circa 1870.

Left: This relic of the Polish saint, St. Stanislaus, is encased in a cruciform holder.

The Polish National Alliance, largest ethnic and Polish fraternal organization in America, was founded in 1880 in Philadelphia to provide services for Polish immigrants in this country. Its home office on North Cicero reports a membership of 317,000 people in 1,402 lodges in 36 states. In addition to insurance benefits for its members, the Alliance supports programs in sports, social activities, and community service.

s. Josephine Rozanska Rzewski, 82, librarian at the PNA, was Recruiting Officer Boston for the Polish Army in France in 1918. She supervises a collection of 00 Polish books, bound periodicals, artifacts, and documents of interest to lish-American history. Among these is a facsimile of the Will of Brigadier General addeus Kosciuszkio, a hero in Poland and in the American Revolutionary War. ecutor of the Will was Thomas Jefferson who called him "the truest son of liberty ave ever known." In it, Kosciuszkio authorizes his friend Jefferson to purchase egroes from among his own or any others and give them Liberty in my name." tues of Kosciuszkio are near the Adler Planetarium in Chicago and in shington, D.C.

Aloysius A. Mazewski, President of the Polish National Alliance.

Left: A portrait of Our Lady of Czestochowa hangs in the narthex of the Mother of Good Counsel Chapel of Felician College.

Below, middle: Sister Mary Bonita, President-Dean of Felician College, meets with a student before the statue of St. Felix of Cantalice, medieval patron of the Capuchin Order, OFM, Cap. The Order of Felician Sisters was named after St. Felix.

Bottom: Students at Felician College meet in the cafeteria between classes. The school is a private, two-year liberal arts college conducted by the Felician Sisters, an order founded in Poland.

Dancers from Chicago's Polish Highlanders Alliance perform on International Peace Day, 1979, in Daley Plaza.

Top of page: Butcher Adam Stachanczyk prepares Polish sausage for smoking in the Bacik Butcher Shop, 2976 N. Milwaukee Ave. on Chicago's heavily Polish Northwest Side.

Above, middle: Grazyna Hucolak slices Polish rye bread in Bacik's where Polish-language newspapers and portraits of Pope John Paul II suitable for framing also are for sale.

Bottom: A gift shop along Milwaukee Avenue offers items imported from Poland and throughout the world.

Credits

EDITOR:	ROBERT E. ZYSKOWSKI
HOUSE EDITOR:	A. JEAN LESHER
PRODUCTION:	LEONARD PRIMER, INC. Designer: Jacqueline Fiedler
HOUSE ART EDITOR:	ROBERT A. SITKOWSKI
MANUFACTURER:	ALDEN PRESS, INC.
SPECIAL ARTIST:	FRANKLIN MCMAHON
PHOTOGRAPHERS:	MILTON and JOAN MANN ROGER MATTINGLY JAMES KILCOYNE KAREN YOPS
PHOTO CREDITS:	Sygma, Black Star, Wide World Photos, Religious News Service, **Chicago Catholic,** Chicago Historical Society, Foto Felici

Front Cover: Fabian-Sygma
Back Cover and Inside Back Cover: Milton and Joan Mann

Other photos from: The Roman Catholic Dioceses of Milwaukee, Peoria, and Springfield; St. Patrick's Church, DePaul University, Loyola University, Mundelein College, and Rosary College

♪ Follett Publishing Company

1010 West Washington Boulevard, Chicago, Illinois 60607   (312) 666-5858

FOLLETT PUBLISHING COMPANY · Chicago

ISBN 0-695-**8134**